Praying
the Rosary
with
St. Paul

PAUL THIGPEN

Praying *the* Rosary *with* St. Paul

Our Sunday Visitor Publishing Division
Our Sunday Visitor, Inc.
Huntington, Indiana 46750

Copyright © 2008 by Our Sunday Visitor Publishing Division, Our Sunday Visitor, Inc. Published 2008.

13 12 11 10 09 08   1 2 3 4 5 6 7 8 9

Our Sunday Visitor Publishing Division
Our Sunday Visitor, Inc.
200 Noll Plaza
Huntington, IN 46750

ISBN: 978-1-59276-553-9 (Inventory No. T835)
LCCN: 2008939126

Cover design: Amanda Miller
Cover art: Shutterstock (rosary image); Scala/Art Resource, NY (St. Paul, detail of the vault mosaics, early Christian, fifth-sixth century C.E.)
Interior design: Sherri L. Hoffman

PRINTED IN THE UNITED STATES OF AMERICA

*For my students at Southern Catholic College,
as they soar upward to Truth
on the wings of faith and reason*

CONTENTS

Why Pray the Rosary
With St. Paul?

To pray the Rosary with St. Paul might seem at first a puzzling notion. After all, the Apostle could not possibly have prayed the Rosary during his life on earth. The custom as we know it today developed a thousand years or more after his time.

Then, too, the Rosary is closely associated with Our Lady. Its name comes from the Latin word *Rosarium* — a garland of roses — and that sweetest of flowers has long been a symbol of Mary. The familiar story of the Virgin Mother's appearance to St. Dominic, instructing him to spread the Rosary devotion, has led to her title "Our Lady of the Rosary." And many of the Rosary mysteries on which we meditate are events from her life.

This particular form of prayer, then, is a supremely Marian form of devotion. Yet St. Paul had very little to say about Jesus' mother in those of his letters that became part of Scripture. We have no clear evidence that he ever even met her. The only biblical text by the Apostle that speaks of Our Lady is a rather general reference in his letter to the Galatians:

> When the fullness of time had come, God sent his Son, born of a woman, born under the law, to ransom those under the law, so that we might receive adoption. (Gal 4:4-5; NAB)

Is it true, then, as some Christians insist, that St. Paul had no interest in Mary, and that we would do well to ignore her, too?

"Paul's Gospel"

In response to that challenge, we should first note that St. Luke the Evangelist was a companion of St. Paul on his apostolic journeys. So some biblical scholars believe that the Gospel of Luke should actually be read as "Paul's Gospel." They say that St. Luke's account of Our Lord's life was shaped by St. Paul's insights into who Christ is and why He came into the world.

If this conclusion is correct, then we should be struck by the fact that St. Luke's story is actually the most "Marian" of the four Gospels. It tells us more than any of the others about Our Lady and her relationship with her divine Son.

In fact, it's in St. Luke's account (which originally included, as its second part, the Book of Acts) that we learn most of what we know about the events in Mary's life featured in the Rosary. In these pages, we find the Annunciation (Lk 1:26-38), the Visitation (Lk 1:39-56), the Nativity (Lk 2:1-20), the Presentation in the Temple (Lk 2:22-39), the Finding of Jesus in the Temple (Lk 2:41-52), and Pentecost (an event at which Mary was present; Acts 1:12-14; 2:1-42).

We might note as well that the most prominent prayer of the Rosary, the Hail Mary, takes most of its words from this same book.

If this is indeed "Paul's Gospel," revealing his vision of Christ, then the Apostle must have had a keen interest in Mary.

Consider as well: How was St. Luke able to learn about even the intimate details of Our Lady's experience with her Son, such as what she was "pondering... in her heart" at His birth (see Lk 2:19)? St. Luke tells us that he relied heavily on eyewitness accounts (see Lk 1:1-4), so some scholars believe that he personally interviewed Mary to gain this information. There are even ancient stories about his painting a portrait of her.

If the Evangelist did in fact know Our Lady, isn't it reasonable to think that he may have introduced her to his close friend and colleague? Since St. Paul hadn't known Our Lord during His earthly lifetime, wouldn't that zealous convert, who devoted his life to teaching people about Christ, have been eager to learn more about Jesus directly from His own mother?

Yet suppose we assume that St. Paul never met Mary, or that St. Luke's careful attention to her doesn't reflect an interest on the part of the Apostle. Even then, we still have good reason to pray the Rosary, with all its Marian prayers and meditations, in the light of St. Paul's words. That reason is found in kernel form in the reference to Mary from St. Paul's own hand that we just cited.

"God sent his Son, born of a woman." This short phrase summarizes the whole Gospel that the great Apostle preached. In Jesus Christ, God Himself became man. He took our human nature and joined it to His own divine nature. Because of that startling historical event, in "the fullness of time," nothing would ever be the same again.

The Word of God who "became flesh and dwelt among us" (Jn 1:14) received His flesh from Mary of Nazareth. That woman, "full of grace" (Lk 1:28), became the first Christian, the model for all the rest. In her immaculate heart, her obedience to God, her devotion to her Son, and her heavenly destiny, we catch a vision of our own vocation to holiness, the summons to a journey that will at last bring us face-to-face with God.

As always, Mary leads us to Jesus. What we discover about her in praying the Rosary teaches us also about her Son and why He came. Yes, it has taken a millennium and more for Christians to unpack this mystery, and we haven't yet finished the task. But St. Paul himself knew that the process would take time, "until we all attain to the unity of the faith and of the knowledge of the Son of God" (Eph 4:13).

In the meantime, the Apostle prayed that we would come to know "the riches of [God's] glorious inheritance in the saints" (Eph 1:18). In the Rosary, we meditate on those riches as we find them in the Queen of Saints: the mother of God's

Son, and the mother of all who "receive adoption" as children of God.

This little book has one purpose, then: to aid those who pray the Rosary to hasten on their journey to Jesus through Mary with the help of St. Paul. No doubt the Apostle is praying right along with us.

PAUL THIGPEN
October 7, 2008
Feast of Our Lady of the Rosary
In the Year of St. Paul

A Note on the Scriptural Texts Used

～

Biblical scholars have debated for many years (as they love to do) about the thirteen books in the New Testament that bear St. Paul's name as author. Many argue that not all of these were actually written by St. Paul. However, when they try to prove which books were his and which were not, they end up contradicting one another. Such confusion at the very least calls into question the reliability of their methods.

On the other hand, the ancient Fathers of the Church, living at a time much closer to that of St. Paul himself, believed that all of these letters were indeed written by him. I stand with them in that traditional view, which nearly all Christians held until modern times, and I have drawn from these epistles most of the scriptural texts for reflection in this book.

The biblical Letter to the Hebrews, however, is admittedly a different matter. It doesn't actually carry St. Paul's name, leaving its authorship open to debate even in ancient times. Since the early centuries of the Church, biblical commentators have noted in particular that its writing style differs in many ways from that of the other books attributed to the Apostle.

Nevertheless, the majority of the ancient Church Fathers believed that the book had in fact come from St. Paul, and various ancient Church councils thought the same. The common assumption was that the variation in writing style could be accounted for in one of two ways: (a) either a disciple of St. Paul had taken notes on the Apostle's teaching and then written it up in his own style or (b) St. Paul had written it in Hebrew, which was then translated into highly polished Greek by St. Luke or another writer.

Centuries later, the great theologian St. Thomas Aquinas was among those who reasoned that Hebrews was St. Paul's handiwork. Later still, when the ecumenical Council of Trent (1545-63) specified the books in the scriptural canon, it declared that there were fourteen Pauline epistles, including Hebrews.

Why would so many commentators, down to the present, continue to conclude that this book has its origins somehow in St. Paul? In part, because so much of its content plainly seems to reflect his thinking as found in the biblical books that bear his name.

At the least, then, we can say this: the Letter to the Hebrews appears to have been written by St. Paul, or put in final form by someone familiar with his teaching, or composed by one of his followers. Whichever is the case, the wisdom of the Apostle shines through it, illuminating our understanding of Jesus Christ.

For this reason, I have decided to include some texts from Hebrews as well. I think you will agree that the passages from that book profoundly enrich these meditations.

Finally, the Book of Acts reports on a number of sermons and speeches of St. Paul. A few of the biblical texts here come from his words recorded there.

THE JOYFUL
MYSTERIES

(Prayed on Mondays and Saturdays)

The Joyful Mysteries of the Rosary focus on events surrounding the conception and birth of Our Lord, as well as one episode from His youth. Not surprisingly, then, Our Lady figures prominently in these mysteries as the loving mother who conceived Him, gave birth to Him, and watched carefully over Him in His young life.

For each of these and the other sets of mysteries, we offer relevant biblical passages for reflection from St. Paul, followed by a brief meditation to prepare us for the Rosary prayers for that mystery. In addition, since the Apostle spoke about the importance of cultivating "the fruit of the Spirit" (Gal 5:22), we note for each mystery a particular spiritual fruit to be sought, along with a brief word about it from St. Paul.

The Joyful Mysteries teach us that the Son of God has become the Son of Mary so that we, too, can become children of God. And that means, St. Paul insists, that we have good reason to "rejoice in the Lord always" (Phil 4:4)!

The First Joyful Mystery

THE ANNUNCIATION OF THE ANGEL GABRIEL TO MARY

Spiritual Fruit: FAITH

Now faith is the assurance of things hoped for, the conviction of things not seen.
HEBREWS 11:1

The Scripture says, "No one who believes in him will be put to shame." . . . For, "every one who calls upon the name of the Lord will be saved."

But how are men to call upon him in whom they have not believed? And how are they to believe in him of whom they have never heard? And how are they to hear without a preacher? And how can men preach unless they are sent? As it is written, "How beautiful are the feet of those who preach good news!" . . . So faith comes from what is heard, and what is heard comes by the preaching of Christ. *(Rom 10:11, 13-15, 17)*

For I long to see you, that I may impart to you some spiritual gift to strengthen you, that is, that we may be mutually encouraged by each other's faith, both yours and mine. *(Rom 1:11-12)*

St. Paul is the great apostle of faith, and Our Lady is the great model of faith.

Faith, the Apostle tells us, comes from hearing Christ preached. When the angel Gabriel, the first messenger to preach Christ, spoke God's word to Mary, great faith rose up within her. In simple, serene confidence she replied, "Let it be to me according to your word" (Lk 1:38).

Faith is being convinced of what we cannot see, St. Paul teaches. Our Lady could not see how, given her virginity, she could conceive a son. But in faith she was convinced that "with God nothing will be impossible" (Lk 1:37), and she believed what she could not see.

The Apostle assures us that if we put our trust in God, we will never be ashamed. Mary knew that bearing a child whose father was not Joseph would subject her to gossip, scorn, and ridicule. But she put her trust in God, and she was not ashamed to bear the Son of God, whatever the price would be.

St. Paul reminds us that those who don't know Jesus need someone to tell them about Him. With faith comes a mission: We who believe are sent by God to tell others the good news of His salvation. And even those who are already believers can be strengthened and encouraged when we share our faith with them.

Once Mary believed the good news about her Son, she went to tell her kinswoman Elizabeth. In that further act of faith, she showed herself to be a "beautiful" messenger of the Gospel, "full of grace."

"We too believe," St. Paul declares, "and so we speak" of the Lord Jesus (2 Cor 4:13). We are called, as Our Lady was, to believe, to trust, and to share our faith.

Silent Reflection
- Our Father
- Ten Hail Marys
- Glory Be
- Fátima Prayer (optional)

The Second Joyful Mystery

THE VISITATION OF OUR LADY
TO ST. ELIZABETH

Spiritual Fruit: KINDNESS

The fruit of the Spirit is . . . kindness.
GALATIANS 5:22

Put on, then, as God's chosen ones, holy and beloved, compassion, kindness, lowliness, meekness, and patience. . . . Let the word of Christ dwell in you richly, as you teach and admonish one another in all wisdom, and as you sing psalms and hymns and spiritual songs with thankfulness in your hearts to God. *(Col 3:12, 16)*

Love one another with brotherly affection; outdo one another in showing honor. . . . Contribute to the needs of the saints; practice hospitality. . . . Rejoice with those who rejoice. *(Rom 12:10, 13, 15a)*

Bear one another's burdens, and so fulfil the law of Christ. *(Gal 6:2)*

When Our Lady heard from the angel that her elderly kinswoman Elizabeth was with child, she "went with haste" to visit her (Lk 1:39). The great kindness of her heart compelled her to hurry to Elizabeth's side to encourage and assist her in her time of need.

The joyful moment of encounter between the two holy women movingly portrays the gracious attitude and conduct that St. Paul tells us will flow from a kind heart.

Mary has come to contribute to the needs of a saint and to rejoice with those who rejoice. Elizabeth is pleased to provide hospitality and is zealous to show honor to the mother of her Lord. Their sisterly affection overflows as they begin their task of bearing one another's burdens, seeking together over the following three months to understand and fulfill the startling will of God in their lives.

The Word, Christ Himself, dwells richly in the womb of Our Lady; and the prophet of that Word, John the Baptist, dwells in Elizabeth's womb. The Holy Spirit stirs within the women, and divine wisdom wells up to their lips, springing out from Mary in a hymn of thankfulness to God.

In all these ways, these two women illustrate St. Paul's instruction to be clothed with "compassion, kindness, lowliness, meekness, and patience." In doing so, they "teach and admonish" us to be, like them, "chosen ones, holy and beloved."

Silent Reflection

- Our Father
- Ten Hail Marys
- Glory Be
- Fátima Prayer (optional)

The Third Joyful Mystery

THE NATIVITY OF OUR LORD

Spiritual Fruit: HUMILITY

*And being found in human form
[Christ] humbled himself.*
PHILIPPIANS 2:8a

Do nothing from selfishness or conceit, but in humility count others better than yourselves. Let each of you look not only to his own interests, but also to the interests of others. Have this mind among yourselves, which was in Christ Jesus, who, though he was in the form of God, did not count equality with God a thing to be grasped, but emptied himself, taking the form of a servant, being born in the likeness of men. *(Phil 2:3-7)*

When the fullness of time had come, God sent his Son, born of a woman, born under the law, to ransom those under the law, so that we might receive adoption. As proof that you are children, God sent the spirit of his Son into our hearts, crying out, "Abba, Father!" . . . My children, for whom I am again in labor until Christ be formed in you! *(Gal 4:4-6, 19; NAB)*

St. Paul observes that when the eternal Son of God laid aside His glory to dwell for a season on earth, He demonstrated much more than His infinite love and power toward us. The act of becoming a man was a stunning display of divine humility as well.

The Voice that had spoken light itself into existence cried out in hunger in the darkness. The Hand that had set the galaxies spinning, and formed the first man from the dust, reached out helplessly for His mother.

If the Creator of the universe could stoop so low to save us, the Apostle reasoned, shouldn't we be willing to humble ourselves for the sake of others?

Nor can we forget the humility of Our Lady that evening. She had willingly endured the humiliation of the neighbors' gossip as they debated who her child's father was. Now she humbled herself to give Him birth among the lowly beasts, laying Him in the box where the cattle had drooled their cud.

What could possibly have compelled God to allow His Son such an ignoble birth? He did it to ransom us, St. Paul tells us, so that we could become His children. The Almighty did the unthinkable so that He could become our Father, through the sacrifice of His divine Son.

The Apostle felt the depths of such a mighty love stirring within himself. Just as Mary had given birth to Jesus, so St. Paul labored to give birth to spiritual children. And he, too, willingly endured frequent humiliations in his ministry for the sake of others. In St. Paul, then, as in Mary, we find a model for living according to the humble mind of Christ.

Silent Reflection

- Our Father
- Ten Hail Marys
- Glory Be
- Fátima Prayer (optional)

The Fourth Joyful Mystery

THE PRESENTATION OF OUR LORD IN THE TEMPLE

Spiritual Fruit: GENEROSITY

You will glorify God . . . by the generosity of your contribution.
2 CORINTHIANS 9:13

"In all things I have shown you that by toiling one must help the weak, remembering the words of the Lord Jesus, how he said, 'It is more blessed to give than to receive.'" *(Acts 20:35)*

For you know the grace of our Lord Jesus Christ, that though he was rich, yet for your sake he became poor, so that by his poverty you might become rich. . . .

. . . He who sows sparingly will also reap sparingly, and he who sows bountifully will also reap bountifully. Each one must do as he has made up his mind, not reluctantly or under compulsion, for God loves a cheerful giver. And God is able to provide you with every blessing in abundance, so that you may always have enough of everything and may provide in abundance for every good work. . . .

He who supplies seed to the sower and bread for food will supply and multiply your resources and increase the harvest of your righteousness. You will be enriched in every way for great generosity, which through us will produce thanksgiving to God. *(2 Cor 8:9; 9:6-8, 10-11)*

When Mary and Joseph presented Jesus in the Temple, they were responding to God's generous Gift with a simple generosity of their own. Heaven had given a Son into their keeping, so they took Him to God's house to give Him back, consecrating the firstborn to the Lord's service.

One detail of this Gospel account that is often overlooked is the type of sacrifice that Our Lady and her blessed husband brought on that day. A "pair of turtledoves, or two young pigeons" (Lk 2:24) was actually the sacrifice, commanded by ancient law, for families who were too poor to afford the sacrificial lamb that was otherwise prescribed (see Lev 12:8).

In later years, the Holy Family might well have had enough income to live comfortably, at least until the death of St. Joseph. But apparently, in the days just after Our Lord's birth, they were a household of limited means — perhaps because of the Roman taxes they had recently been obliged to pay.

St. Paul offers a pointed reminder to all those who might be reluctant to give generously to the needy: Our Lord gave up the unspeakable riches of His heavenly glory to become poor for our sakes. Through His voluntary poverty, we now have access to the spiritual riches of heaven, however few our material possessions may be.

Like the Holy Family, then, we can give generously and joyfully, because God has already given to us. When we do, St. Paul insists, the "seed" we sow will enrich us further still with an abundant spiritual harvest. The Lord's words that St. Paul reported become true in our lives: "It is more blessed to give than to receive."

Silent Reflection

- Our Father
- Ten Hail Marys
- Glory Be
- Fátima Prayer (optional)

The Fifth Joyful Mystery

THE FINDING OF THE CHILD JESUS IN THE TEMPLE

Spiritual Fruit: WISDOM

I strive for you . . . to have . . . Christ, in whom are hidden all the treasures of wisdom and knowledge.
COLOSSIANS 2:1, 2, 3

Christ [is] the power of God and the wisdom of God. For the foolishness of God is wiser than men, and the weakness of God is stronger than men.

For consider your call, brethren; not many of you were wise according to the flesh, not many were powerful, not many were of noble birth; but God chose what is foolish in the world to shame the wise, God chose what is weak in the world to shame the strong, God chose what is low and despised in the world, even things that are not, to bring to nothing things that are, so that no flesh might boast in the presence of God. He is the source of your life in Christ Jesus, whom God made our wisdom, our righteousness and sanctification and redemption; therefore, as it is written, "Let him who boasts, boast of the Lord." *(1 Cor 1:24-31)*

Young Jesus stayed behind in Jerusalem after Passover, without letting Mary and Joseph know where He was. As they searched anxiously for Him, they would have worried that, not yet fully a man, he was too weak to protect Himself. They may even have been tempted to think that He had acted foolishly in getting separated from them.

When they finally located Him, they learned that their fears about His weakness were unfounded. And when He told them that He had to be about His Father's business, they knew that His actions had been anything but foolish.

Even in His youth, Jesus was beginning to challenge the expectations others had for Him. His parents "were astonished"; the teachers in the temple "were amazed at his understanding" (Lk 2:47-48).

The lad's later years only made matters worse for those who failed to recognize who He truly was. St. Paul, a Pharisee, was especially scandalized by Christ's life. How could any intelligent person believe that someone executed as a criminal by the Romans was Israel's divine Savior? Could God be so foolish, or His Messiah so weak?

When St. Paul finally encountered Jesus Christ on the road to Damascus, his understanding of heaven's plan was revolutionized. The Power of God threw him to the ground, and the Wisdom of God enlightened his mind. He was converted.

Like the Apostle, we, too, must be converted, again and again, from ways of thinking that reject God's wise plan for our lives, even when it doesn't make sense to us for now. Like Mary, the "Seat of Wisdom," we must listen to what her Son says, and then ponder it carefully in our hearts (see Lk 2:51).

Silent Reflection

- Our Father
- Ten Hail Marys
- Glory Be
- Fátima Prayer (optional)

THE LUMINOUS MYSTERIES

(Prayed on Thursdays)

The Luminous Mysteries of the Rosary, or Mysteries of Light, focus on events during the years of Jesus' public ministry. They begin with His baptism in the Jordan and end with the institution of the Holy Eucharist at the Last Supper, on the night He was betrayed.

Our Lady appears less explicitly in these events, except for her prominent role in the miracle of the feast at Cana. Even so, we can speculate that she may well have stood nearby when her Son was baptized and when He preached the Gospel of the kingdom of God. No doubt she was closely united with Him in prayer when He experienced the Transfiguration and when He celebrated the first Eucharist.

The Luminous Mysteries call us to meditate on Christ, the Light of the world, so that we can, as St. Paul declares, "walk as children of light" (Eph 5:8).

The First Luminous Mystery

THE BAPTISM OF OUR LORD IN THE JORDAN

Spiritual Fruit: REPENTANCE

"I did not shrink from . . . testifying . . . of repentance to God and of faith in our Lord Jesus Christ."
ACTS 20:20-21

Are we to continue in sin that grace may abound? By no means! How can we who died to sin still live in it? Do you not know that all of us who have been baptized into Christ Jesus were baptized into his death? We were buried therefore with him by baptism into death, so that as Christ was raised from the dead by the glory of the Father, we too might walk in newness of life. . . .

So you also must consider yourselves dead to sin and alive to God in Christ Jesus. . . .

Do not yield your members to sin as instruments of wickedness, but yield yourselves to God as men who have been brought from death to life, and your members to God as instruments of righteousness. *(Rom 6:1-4, 11, 13)*

Do you presume upon the riches of [God's] kindness and forbearance and patience? Do you not know that God's kindness is meant to lead you to repentance? *(Rom 2:4)*

The baptism that St. John administered to the crowds at the Jordan River was a "baptism of repentance for the forgiveness of sins" (Lk 3:3). Our Lord, of course, had no need of repentance, because He had no sins to be forgiven. Yet He humbly submitted himself to baptism as an act of solidarity with the sinful people He came to save.

Our sacramental baptism powerfully washes away sin in a way that John's baptism never could. Yet St. Paul tells us that it, too, should be in one sense a baptism of repentance. Whenever we fall into sin, we should look back to those baptismal waters and recall what they mean.

As the waters cleansed us, we actually took part in the saving death of Jesus so that we could die to sin and live new life in Him. If we are now new creatures in Christ, we must let go of the old way of life that is opposed to God. The baptismal font was its tomb, and there we must leave that rotting corpse of sin that was once ours.

In remembering our baptism, the Apostle says, we should remember as well God's kindness in giving up His Son to redeem us. That patient, forbearing kindness should provoke us to repent — to turn away from everything that would break His heart and keep us from living the eternal life Jesus died to give us.

Through constantly renewing our repentance in this way, we conform our lives more closely to Christ, and we fulfill the vocation to holiness we received when we were baptized into Him.

Silent Reflection

- Our Father
- Ten Hail Marys
- Glory Be
- Fátima Prayer (optional)

The Second Luminous Mystery

THE MIRACLE AT THE
WEDDING FEAST IN CANA

Spiritual Fruit: OBEDIENCE

*Now to him who is able to strengthen you . . .
to bring about the obedience of faith . . .
be glory for evermore.*
ROMANS 16:25, 26, 27

I will not venture to speak of anything except
what Christ has wrought through me to win
obedience from the Gentiles, by word and
deed, by the power of signs and wonders, by
the power of the Holy Spirit. *(Rom 15:18-19)*

Therefore, my beloved, as you have always
obeyed, so now, not only as in my presence
but much more in my absence, work out
your own salvation with fear and trembling,
for God is at work in you, both to will and
to work for his good pleasure.

Do all things without grumbling or questioning, that you may be blameless and innocent, children of God without blemish in the midst of a crooked and perverse generation, among whom you shine as lights in the world, holding fast the word of life. *(Phil 2:12-16)*

According to the Gospel, Jesus' miracle at the wedding feast in Cana — turning water into wine for the guests — was "the first of his signs ... and manifested his glory; and his disciples believed in him" (Jn 2:11).

Now, a *sign* is something that points beyond itself to what is greater. Like all the miraculous signs Christ performed, the wondrous wine was not the end in itself; it pointed to Christ. It bore witness to who He was, and that witness planted within His disciples the first seeds of faith.

Mary's role in this miracle was critical. Not only did she hint to her Son that He could rescue the wedding party from embarrassment, but she also secured the help of the servants by instructing them to obey Him: "Do whatever he tells you" (Jn 2:5).

Her words were born in an act of faith. She had every confidence that Jesus could do what she asked of Him, and she trusted in His goodness.

In this situation, as in so many, faith gave birth to faith by way of obedience. Our Lady's trust made possible the servants' faithful cooperation. Their cooperation made possible the miraculous sign. And the sign made it possible for Christ's disciples to believe in Him.

Our Lord's miracles did not cease, of course, with His ascension into heaven. They continued in the life of the Church, as St. Paul's testimony affirms. Then, as before, they were "signs and wonders" that pointed to Christ, works of faith that led to obedience, so that He would be glorified.

In our lives, too, "the obedience of faith" will manifest Christ. When we work for God's good pleasure "without grumbling or questioning," the Apostle assures us, we become "lights in the world" — signs pointing to Him, no less powerful than the miracles of old.

Silent Reflection

- Our Father
- Ten Hail Marys
- Glory Be
- Fátima Prayer (optional)

The Third Luminous Mystery

THE PROCLAMATION OF THE KINGDOM OF GOD

Spiritual Fruit: RIGHTEOUSNESS

*The kingdom of God . . . [is] righteousness and peace
and joy in the Holy Spirit.*
ROMANS 14:17

The Father . . . has qualified us to share in
the inheritance of the saints in light. He has
delivered us from the dominion of darkness
and transferred us to the kingdom of his
beloved Son, in whom we have redemption,
the forgiveness of sins. *(Col 1:12-14)*

Do you not know that the unrighteous will
not inherit the kingdom of God? Do not be
deceived; neither the immoral, nor idolaters,
nor adulterers, nor [homosexual offenders],
nor thieves, nor the greedy, nor drunkards,
nor revilers, nor robbers will inherit the
kingdom of God. And such were some of

you. But you were washed, you were sancti-
fied, you were justified in the name of the
Lord Jesus Christ and in the Spirit of our
God. *(1 Cor 6:9-11)*

To be righteous is to be rightly related — to
God, to ourselves, and to others. To be unrighteous
is to be disordered in all these relationships.

St. Paul tells us that righteousness is a "peace-
ful fruit" (Heb 12:11) — that is, when we are
rightly ordered, tranquility results. We are in har-
mony with God, ourselves, and others. But the
disorder of unrighteousness leads to chaos and
misery, both within us and all around us.

In the kingdom of God — the reign of God —
right relationships prevail, because all things are
well ordered there by the rule of the rightful King.
And if His good will orders all things rightly, then
to pray "Thy kingdom come" is indeed to pray
"Thy will be done, on earth as it is in heaven" (Mt
6:10).

When Jesus proclaimed the coming of God's
kingdom, the Beatitudes were an essential part of
His proclamation. Some have, in fact, called
them "the charter of the kingdom of God." At
the foundation of that charter lies this precious

promise: "Blessed are those who hunger and thirst for righteousness, for they shall be satisfied" (Mt 5:6).

In this light, we can see why the Apostle warns us that the unrighteous will not inherit the kingdom of God. They have rejected the reign of His beloved Son, and so they live in "the dominion of darkness," confused and stumbling, in perpetual conflict.

Even so, St. Paul offers hope: "Such were some of you" — but no longer. Through God's grace, we can learn to "walk in a manner worthy of God, who calls [us] into his own kingdom and glory" (1 Thess 2:12).

Silent Reflection

- Our Father
- Ten Hail Marys
- Glory Be
- Fátima Prayer (optional)

The Fourth Luminous Mystery

THE TRANSFIGURATION OF OUR LORD

Spiritual Fruit: GLORY

We rejoice in our hope of sharing the glory of God.
ROMANS 5:2

We are children of God, and if children, then heirs, heirs of God and fellow heirs with Christ, provided we suffer with him in order that we may also be glorified with him.

I consider that the sufferings of this present time are not worth comparing with the glory that is to be revealed to us. *(Rom 8:16-18)*

And we all, with unveiled face, beholding the glory of the Lord, are being changed into his likeness from one degree of glory to another. . . . For it is God who said, "Let light shine out of darkness," who has shone in our hearts to give the light of the knowledge of the glory of God in the face of Christ. . . .

So we do not lose heart. . . . For this slight momentary affliction is preparing for us an eternal weight of glory beyond all comparison, because we look not to the things that are seen but to the things that are unseen; for the things that are seen are transient, but the things that are unseen are eternal. *(2 Cor 3:18; 4:6, 16, 17-18)*

In the dazzling transfiguration of Jesus, we catch a glimpse of the glory He had laid aside to descend from heaven, and the glory He now shares there, once again, with His Father and the Holy Spirit. Peter, James, and John, awed by the splendor, understandably wanted to stay on the mountaintop, basking in the brilliance.

But they could not linger. The demoniac was waiting down in the valley, desperately in need of Christ's power. And St. Luke tells us that when Jesus healed the boy, in that moment — as in the Transfiguration — "the majesty of God" was revealed (Lk 9:43).

Soon after, Jesus warned the disciples that His passion and death were coming, and that He would be raised from the dead (see Mt 17:22-23). To enjoy the glory that awaited Him, He first had to suffer.

St. Paul exults that those who are in Christ will one day share His glory. But he affirms that for us, too, suffering precedes the glory and actually prepares us for it. In fact, our daily triumphs over evil in this world, like Jesus' victory over the demon in the valley, can themselves manifest God's glory to those with eyes to see it.

In the meantime, those glimpses of Christ's shining face in the midst of our darkness have the power to transform us. The more we reflect His grace, the more we become like Him, moving us closer to that day when we will be perfectly like Him in heaven, where "we shall see him as he is. And every one who thus hopes in him purifies himself as he is pure" (1 Jn 3:2-3).

Silent Reflection

- Our Father
- Ten Hail Marys
- Glory Be
- Fátima Prayer (optional)

The Fifth Luminous Mystery

THE INSTITUTION OF THE EUCHARIST

Spiritual Fruit: **UNION WITH CHRIST**

*He who is united with the Lord
becomes one spirit with him.*
1 CORINTHIANS 6:17

For I received from the Lord what I also delivered to you, that the Lord Jesus on the night when he was betrayed took bread, and when he had given thanks, he broke it, and said, "This is my body which is for you. Do this in remembrance of me." In the same way also the chalice, after supper, saying, "This chalice is the new covenant in my blood. Do this, as often as you drink it, in remembrance of me." For as often as you eat this bread and drink the chalice, you proclaim the Lord's death until he comes. *(1 Cor 11:23-26)*

Indeed I count everything as loss because of the surpassing worth of knowing Christ Jesus my Lord. For his sake I have suffered the loss of all things, and count them as refuse, in order that I may gain Christ ... that I may know him and the power of his resurrection, and may share his sufferings, becoming like him in his death, that if possible I may attain the resurrection from the dead.

Not that I have already obtained this or am already perfect; but I press on to make it my own, because Christ Jesus has made me his own. *(Phil 3:8, 10-12)*

When St. Paul speaks about knowing Christ and sharing His life, we are hearing a cry from the depths of his heart. It shouts out the consuming passion that drove him forward and kept him alive, from the day of his conversion to the day of his martyrdom. For the Apostle, the desire to be with his Lord, fully and forever united with Him, was a ravenous hunger, a raging thirst.

Only in heaven, he knew, would his yearning finally come to an end, his heart's deepest longing fulfilled. But even in this life, St. Paul could begin to satisfy the hunger and to quench the thirst with the heavenly Banquet first prepared by Jesus on the night He was betrayed. At the altar of the Lord, the sacred Body and Blood brought the Apostle into a true communion with Jesus Christ. There, St. Paul tasted his Master's life and death, suffering and glory, making it all his own.

Each "remembrance" of the Lord at that Table united St. Paul more closely with Christ, deepening his gratitude for the Sacrifice in which he now shared. But it also pressed the Apostle to look forward in hope, eager for the day when his Lord would return and gather together His people so that they would "always be with the Lord" (1 Thess 4:17).

Like St. Paul, we must daily press on to the goal of possessing Christ fully as our own. And we must press in to that most holy Altar, to feed on the Eucharist, which gives us even now a foretaste of the union awaiting all those He has made His own.

Silent Reflection

- Our Father
- Ten Hail Marys
- Glory Be
- Fátima Prayer (optional)

THE SORROWFUL MYSTERIES

(Prayed on Tuesdays and Fridays)

The Sorrowful Mysteries of the Rosary take us into the terrifying, yet consoling, events at the climax of Christ's earthly life.

They are terrifying, because in them we see the Son of God humiliated, tortured, and executed. They are consoling, because in them we see just how wondrous the love of God the Father is for us.

Through these meditations we encounter "a man of sorrows ... acquainted with grief ... wounded for our transgressions ... bruised for our iniquities" (Is 53:3, 5). If He bore our sorrows, then we must unite ourselves with His sorrows, grieving over our sins that brought Him to the cross. When we do, St. Paul tells us, such "godly grief produces a repentance that leads to salvation and brings no regret" (2 Cor 7:10).

The First Sorrowful Mystery

THE AGONY IN THE GARDEN

Spiritual Fruit: PEACE

*[God reconciled] to himself all things, . . . making
peace by the blood of his cross.*
COLOSSIANS 1:20

In the days of his flesh, Jesus offered up
prayers and supplications, with loud cries
and tears, to him who was able to save him
from death, and he was heard for his godly
fear. Although he was a Son, he learned
obedience through what he suffered; and
being made perfect he became the source
of eternal salvation to all who obey him.
(Heb 5:7-9)

Have no anxiety about anything, but in
everything by prayer and supplication with
thanksgiving let your requests be made
known to God. And the peace of God,
which passes all understanding, will keep

your hearts and your minds in Christ Jesus.
(Phil 4:6-7)

It seems a paradox that one spiritual fruit of meditation on Christ's agony in the garden should be peace. How could we possibly find peace by remembering how our Savior struggled on that darkest of nights, when He was so tormented by the prospect of His passion that He actually sweated drops of blood?

The paradox is resolved when we consider what Our Lord accomplished through His passion and death after the season of struggle was complete. Through that infinite sacrifice, our sinful race, alienated from God and under His just condemnation, was reconciled to Him at last. The blood of His cross, St. Paul declares, opened the way for us to find peace with God.

Having peace *with* God, we can learn to enjoy the peace *of* God. Jesus "offered up prayers and supplications," the Apostle notes, and — trusting in the One who could save Him — the Son at last rested peacefully in the perfect will of His Father. And we can do the same.

When we find ourselves struggling in our own Gethsemane, our cup filled with agony and sorrow, St. Paul calls us to imitate Christ. "By prayer and supplication with thanksgiving," we must lay open our hearts to God, trusting in Him. When we do, we may not understand our circumstances any better, or the reasons why heaven has allowed them. But "the peace ... which passes all understanding" will nevertheless allow us to rest, with Christ, in the bosom of His Father.

Silent Reflection

- Our Father
- Ten Hail Marys
- Glory Be
- Fátima Prayer (optional)

The Second Sorrowful Mystery

THE SCOURGING AT THE PILLAR

Spiritual Fruit: SELF-CONTROL

*For God did not give us a spirit of timidity but
a spirit of power and love and self-control.*
2 TIMOTHY 1:7

I do not understand my own actions. For I
do not do what I want, but I do the very
thing I hate. . . . I can will what is right, but
I cannot do it. . . . Wretched man that I am!
Who will deliver me. . . ? Thanks be to God
through Jesus Christ our Lord! *(Rom 7:15,
18, 24, 25)*

Be temperate, dignified, self-controlled,
sound in faith, love and endurance. . . . For
the grace of God has appeared, saving all
and training us to reject godless ways and
worldly desires and to live temperately,
justly, and devoutly in this age, as we await
the blessed hope, the appearance of the

glory of the great God and of our savior Jesus Christ, who gave himself for us to deliver us from all lawlessness and to cleanse for himself a people as his own, eager to do what is good. *(Titus 2:2, 11-14; NAB)*

When St. Peter brandished his sword to protect Jesus from arrest in Gethsemane, Our Lord rebuked him with a sobering reminder: "Do you think that I cannot appeal to my Father, and he will at once send me more than twelve legions of angels?" (Mt 26:53).

If we keep that statement in mind as we meditate on Jesus' passion and death, we begin to have some notion of how great were His powers of self-control. At the pillar, as each terrible lash laid open His flesh, exposing His nerves, He could have ended the torment with a summons to the heavenly hosts.

But He refused such aid. He endured the horror. And He did it all to rescue us from sin, St. Paul says, to make us His own — a people who can overcome temptation because they are eager to do all good.

The Apostle was brutally honest in confessing that he himself knew what it is like to lack self-control. In his own struggle to do the right and refuse the wrong, he had come to the edge of despair. But he had called out to his Lord to rescue him, and his Lord had indeed come to the rescue.

St. Paul discovered that self-control is control *of* the self, but not *by* the self. In ourselves, we are powerless to resist sin. But when we learn to yield ourselves to the Savior, allowing Him to control us, then "the grace of God" appears.

That cleansing "grace is sufficient" for us, St. Paul insists, for God's "power is made perfect in weakness" (2 Cor 12:9). As He trains us "to reject godless ways and worldly desires," Christ's strength — so manifest in the scourging at the pillar — becomes our own.

Silent Reflection

- Our Father
- Ten Hail Marys
- Glory Be
- Fátima Prayer (optional)

The Third Sorrowful Mystery

THE CROWNING WITH THORNS

Spiritual Fruit: MERCY

As the Lord has forgiven you,
so you also must forgive.
COLOSSIANS 3:13

We see Jesus, who for a little while was made lower than the angels, crowned with glory and honor because of the suffering of death, so that by the grace of God he might taste death for every one. *(Heb 2:9)*

I thank him who has given me strength for this, Christ Jesus our Lord, . . . though I formerly blasphemed and persecuted and insulted him; but I received mercy because I had acted ignorantly in unbelief, and the grace of our Lord overflowed for me with the faith and love that are in Jesus Christ. The saying is sure and worthy of full acceptance, that Christ Jesus came into the world to save sinners. And I am the foremost of sinners; but I received mercy for this reason, that in me, as the foremost, Jesus Christ might display his perfect patience for an example to those who were to believe in him for eternal life. *(1 Tim 1:12, 13-16)*

When St. Paul looked at Jesus crowned with thorns, he saw Him also crowned with glory and honor in heaven. Both the humiliation and the triumph, he insisted, were part of God's plan. Because Our Lord "tasted death" for us all, He can now spread the Table of eternal life and invite us to taste the heavenly Banquet.

When St. Paul looked at those responsible for the crown of thorns, he saw himself among them. Our Lord's executioners had cruelly tormented and mocked the Savior. The Apostle confessed that, by his mistreatment of Jesus' followers, as a zealous young Pharisee he, too, had "blasphemed and persecuted and insulted" Christ.

Nevertheless, St. Paul declared, God's mercy had prevailed. Jesus had prayed for those who hated Him, as they surrounded the cross: "Father, forgive them; for they know not what they do" (Lk 23:34). In the same way, St. Paul himself had "received mercy because [he] had acted ignorantly in unbelief."

"The foremost of sinners": St. Paul knew he had committed sins that merited eternal death. But God had forgiven him and offered him instead the priceless gift of eternal life. How, then, could St. Paul possibly fail to forgive others their sins against him? How could any of us, in view of God's mercy, refuse to show mercy?

Do we see ourselves, as the Apostle did, among those who crowned Our Lord with thorns? If so, we must remember that "blessed are the merciful, for they shall obtain mercy" (Mt 5:7).

God is "rich in mercy," St. Paul tells us, displaying "the immeasurable riches of his grace in kindness toward us in Christ Jesus" (Eph 2:4, 7). That grace of forgiveness must overflow through us to others.

Silent Reflection

- Our Father
- Ten Hail Marys
- Glory Be
- Fátima Prayer (optional)

The Fourth Sorrowful Mystery

THE CARRYING OF THE CROSS

Spiritual Fruit: JOY

Rejoice in the Lord always; again I will say, Rejoice.
PHILIPPIANS 4:4

Therefore, since we are surrounded by so great a cloud of witnesses, let us also lay aside every weight, and sin which clings so closely, and let us run with perseverance the race that is set before us, looking to Jesus the pioneer and perfecter of our faith, who for the joy that was set before him endured the cross, despising the shame, and is seated at the right hand of the throne of God. *(Heb 12:1-2)*

We rejoice in our sufferings, knowing that suffering produces endurance, and endurance produces character, and character produces hope, and hope does not disappoint us, because God's love has been poured into our hearts through the Holy Spirit who has been given to us. . . . Rejoice in your hope, be patient in tribulation, be constant in prayer. *(Rom 5:3-5; 12:12)*

Joy, like peace, may seem at first an unlikely fruit of meditation on Our Lord's passion. But if we think that rejoicing and suffering are incompatible, St. Paul's words should press us to reconsider their relationship.

Too often joy is confused with happiness. But the two are not at all the same.

On the one hand, *happiness* is the sense of satisfaction we feel when we obtain something we have desired. For that reason, the pursuit of happiness in this life is the unhappiest of pursuits. Our desires change. We often get what we want, but then we find ourselves wanting something else.

In heaven, our happiness will be perfect and eternal, because every good thing we could ever want will be possessed by us when we fully possess God, and are fully possessed by Him. But until then, our happiness will be fleeting.

Joy, on the other hand, is the sense of delight that springs up within us at the sight of something or someone we love. So even when we are profoundly unhappy — even when we are suffering terribly — we can have joy, if we look to the One who is joy to behold.

St. Paul tells us that Jesus was able to endure the agony of carrying the cross because of "the joy that was set before him." What did He see lying ahead that gave Him such powerful joy?

John's Gospel tells us that as He approached His passion, Jesus knew that He was on His way "to the Father" (Jn 13:1). Focusing on that glorious destiny with the One He loved above all things filled Him with joy, despite the pain.

St. Paul urges us to rejoice in suffering, because we, too, have the hope of following Our Lord to heaven. If we want joy to rise up in our hearts, we must look with love and hope, past the trials of the day, to the face of Jesus — "the pioneer and perfecter of our faith," who waits for us at the end of our journey.

Silent Reflection

- Our Father
- Ten Hail Marys
- Glory Be
- Fátima Prayer (optional)

The Fifth Sorrowful Mystery

THE CRUCIFIXION OF OUR LORD

Spiritual Fruit: LOVE

So faith, hope, love abide, these three;
but the greatest of these is love.
1 CORINTHIANS 13:13

I have been crucified with Christ; it is no longer I who live, but Christ who lives in me; and the life I now live in the flesh I live by faith in the Son of God, who loved me and gave himself for me. *(Gal 2:20)*

God shows his love for us in that while we were yet sinners Christ died for us. *(Rom 5:8)*

Love is patient and kind; love is not jealous or boastful; it is not arrogant or rude. Love does not insist on its own way; it is not irritable or resentful; it does not rejoice at wrong, but rejoices in the right. Love bears all things, believes all things, hopes all things, endures all things.

Love never ends. *(1 Cor 13:4-8)*

One of the most beautiful passages in all of sacred Scripture is St. Paul's magnificent portrayal of love in his first letter to the Corinthians (chapter 13). Line upon line, he adds another and yet another brushstroke to the masterpiece, as he skillfully paints that most excellent of virtues.

When he is done, the portrait that emerges is the face of Christ crucified. For "God shows his love for us" in the passion and death of His Son.

While Jesus' tormenters were enraged and brutal, He was patient and kind. All around Him, His enemies were jealous and boastful, arrogant and rude, angry and resentful; but He was not.

He did not insist on His own way. He did not seek to escape.

The mob surrounding Him took pleasure in His agony, rejoicing at the greatest injustice of all time. But He turned a bloody face to the penitent thief at His side and rejoiced that the converted sinner would join Him that day in Paradise.

In fathomless love for His Father and for us, Jesus bore all things, believed all things, hoped all things, and endured all things. And His deathless love will never end.

"The Son of God," St. Paul exulted, "loved me and gave himself for me." Not just for the *world,* but for *me.*

In gratitude, I now give myself for Him. I am crucified with Christ. Everything within me that opposes love must be nailed to the cross: selfishness, pride, envy, greed, and all the rest. Only then can Jesus live His life of love in me.

Silent Reflection

- Our Father
- Ten Hail Marys
- Glory Be
- Fátima Prayer (optional)

THE GLORIOUS MYSTERIES

(Prayed on Wednesdays and Sundays)

In the Glorious Mysteries of the Rosary, we soar upward from the depths of hell to the heights of heaven. The tomb could not hold Jesus Christ, the Lord of Life. Death is defeated, and in that conquest we celebrate our own triumph.

Our Lady appears once again prominently in these mysteries, and for good reason. God's promises to those who are in Christ are first and most beautifully fulfilled in her. In her assumption and coronation, we rejoice to see displayed in our Blessed Mother the hope offered in her Son's resurrection, the victory accomplished in His ascension, and the power of the Holy Spirit descending at Pentecost.

St. Paul wrote often of glory, and his frequent meditation on its mystery filled him with unshakable hope. "God chose to make known," he thrilled to declare, "the riches of the glory of this mystery, which is Christ in you, the hope of glory" (Col 1:27).

The First Glorious Mystery

THE RESURRECTION OF OUR LORD

Spiritual Fruit: HOPE

*Seize the hope set before us . . . a sure and
steadfast anchor of the soul.*
HEBREWS 6:18, 19

If Christ has not been raised, your faith is
futile and you are still in your sins. Then
those who have fallen asleep in Christ have
perished. If for this life only we have hoped in
Christ, we are of all men most to be pitied.

But in fact Christ has been raised from
the dead, the first fruits of those who have
fallen asleep. For as by a man came death,
by a man has come also the resurrection of
the dead. For as in Adam all die, so also in
Christ shall all be made alive. But each in
his own order: Christ the first fruits, then at
his coming those who belong to Christ.
(1 Cor 15:17-23)

May the God of hope fill you with all joy and peace in believing, so that by the power of the Holy Spirit you may abound in hope. *(Rom 15:13)*

"Fear of death," St. Paul observes, can make us "subject to lifelong bondage" (Heb 2:15). We fear, not just our own death, but the death of all we love.

Precious family members and friends, pleasant activities, treasured places. A child's innocent laughter, a glorious symphony, the splendor of sunrise over the seashore. All these will pass away.

We will one day leave this world, and this world itself will one day come to an end. Does the awareness of these realities bind us in chains of dread — or liberate us with a thrill of hope?

If not for the resurrection of Christ, the Apostle reminds us, we would have good reason to fear death. This life would be meaningless, only a curious, passing shadow.

But Our Lord has indeed been raised from the dead, and His resurrection can be ours as well, the doorway to new, eternal life in heaven. The Son of God became the Son of man so that "through death he might destroy him who has the power of death, that is, the devil, and deliver all those" who are bound by the fear of death (Heb 2:14-15).

The enemy of our souls has been defeated, but he seeks to undermine our confidence in God and lead us to despair. One of his strategies is to tempt us to focus all our affections on this world so that we will fear death above all things — and become his captive.

For that reason, St. Paul urges us to "seize the hope set before us," the promise of resurrection, as a guard for our thoughts against such temptation. If we do, then we will know what it means to "put on . . . for a helmet the hope of salvation" (1 Thess 5:8).

Silent Reflection

- Our Father
- Ten Hail Marys
- Glory Be
- Fátima Prayer (optional)

The Second Glorious Mystery

THE ASCENSION OF OUR LORD INTO HEAVEN

Spiritual Fruit: VICTORY

But thanks be to God, who gives us the victory through our Lord Jesus Christ.
1 CORINTHIANS 15:57

I do not cease to give thanks for you, remembering you in my prayers, that the God of our Lord Jesus Christ, the Father of glory, may give you a spirit of wisdom and of revelation in the knowledge of him, having the eyes of your hearts enlightened, that you may know what is the hope to which he has called you, what are the riches of his glorious inheritance in the saints, and what is the immeasurable greatness of his power in us who believe, according to the working of his great might which he accomplished in Christ when he raised him from the dead and made him sit at his right hand in the heavenly places, far above all rule and authority and power and dominion, and above every name that is named, not only in this age but also in that which is to come; and he has put all things under his feet and has made him head over all things for the Church, which is his body, the fulness of him who fills all in all. *(Eph 1:16-23)*

When Our Lord ascended into heaven, the apostles watched as "a cloud took him out of their sight" (Acts 1:9). For the time being, His departure was all they could see of what happened that day. They could not watch as He arrived at His destination.

St. Paul was not present at Jesus' ascension. But God granted him wisdom to understand the reality of what had actually taken place, though hidden from earthly view.

In the Ascension, Our Lord returned to the glory of heaven, which He had known before He came to earth. But it was much more than a simple homecoming, St. Paul teaches us. While on earth, He had conquered sin, death, and Satan on our behalf. So now He was ascending as a triumphant King, with every enemy vanquished "under his feet."

We should thrill to realize that to speak of Jesus' having "feet" in heaven is not simply figurative language. Having taken our human nature and joined it to His own, He has glorified it, but He will never abandon it. The One who rules at God's right hand, then, has human hands and feet, with glorious battle scars. He is one of our own — the Head of the Church, which is His body.

St. Paul presses us to recognize the tremendous implications of this truth. If our Head, the representative of our race, is enthroned in glory as the all-conquering King, then we are there with Him. "God . . . raised us up with him," insists the Apostle, "and made us sit with him in the heavenly places in Christ Jesus" (Eph 2:4, 6).

Because we are seated with Christ, who "intercedes for us" there (Rom 8:34), we can rise above the difficult circumstances of our daily lives, no matter how dire. Trials, distress, persecution, hunger, poverty, peril, danger — "in all these things," the Apostle declares, "we are more than conquerors through him who loved us" (Rom 8:37).

Silent Reflection

- Our Father
- Ten Hail Marys
- Glory Be
- Fátima Prayer (optional)

The Third Glorious Mystery

THE DESCENT OF THE HOLY SPIRIT AT PENTECOST

Spiritual Fruit: POWER

Our gospel came to you not only in word, but also in power and in the Holy Spirit and with full conviction.
1 THESSALONIANS 1:5

Now there are varieties of gifts, but the same Spirit; and there are varieties of service, but the same Lord; and there are varieties of working, but it is the same God who inspires them all in every one. To each is given the manifestation of the Spirit for the common good. To one is given through the Spirit the utterance of wisdom, and to another the utterance of knowledge according to the same Spirit, to another faith by the same Spirit, to another gifts of healing by the one Spirit, to another the work of miracles, to another prophecy, to another the ability to distinguish between spirits, to another various kinds of tongues, to another the interpretation of tongues. All these are inspired by one and the same Spirit, who apportions to each one individually as he wills. *(1 Cor 12:4-11)*

Now to him who by the power at work within us is able to do far more abundantly than all that we ask or think, to him be glory in the Church and in Christ Jesus to all generations, for ever and ever. Amen. *(Eph 3:20-21)*

Jesus' last promise to the apostles before His ascension was to send the Holy Spirit so that they would be "clothed with power from on high" (Lk 24:49). On the day of Pentecost, that promise was gloriously fulfilled. Like the rush of a mighty wind and tongues of fire, the Spirit descended on the new Church. Those who were clothed with that power were never the same again.

As the ranks of new believers multiplied and diversified, so did the Spirit's powerful gifts. By the time St. Paul was writing to the Christians at

Corinth in Asia Minor, the works of Our Lord through His extended body, the Church, had spread out far beyond His native land. In the power of the Spirit, believers were working miracles, prophesying, teaching, healing, administering the Church, and much more (see 1 Cor 12:8-10, 28-30).

The Apostle praised God for these spiritual graces. But he had to admonish those in the Church who enjoyed them not to let their diversity become a source of pride and division. However great their differences of background, or their variety of gifts, they had all been privileged to "drink of one Spirit," and by that one Spirit they had all been "baptized into one body" (1 Cor 12:13).

The power of the Spirit is needed to do the work of the Church, St. Paul teaches. But His mighty gifts to us and through us should never lead us to boast, nor to conclude that we have no need of the gifts He has given others. If instead we use our gifts "for the common good," then the Spirit's power at work within us will be able to do "far more abundantly than what we ask or think."

Silent Reflection

- Our Father
- Ten Hail Marys
- Glory Be
- Fátima Prayer (optional)

The Fourth Glorious Mystery

THE ASSUMPTION OF OUR LADY INTO HEAVEN

Spiritual Fruit: ENDURANCE

If we endure, we shall also reign with him.
2 TIMOTHY 2:12

Behold! I tell you a mystery. We shall not all sleep, but we shall all be changed, in a moment, in the twinkling of an eye, at the last trumpet. For the trumpet will sound, and the dead will be raised imperishable, and we shall be changed. For this perishable nature must put on the imperishable, and this mortal nature must put on immortality. *(1 Cor 15:51-53)*

I have fought the good fight, I have finished the race, I have kept the faith. From now on there is laid up for me the crown of righteousness, which the Lord, the righteous judge, will award to me on that Day, and not only to me but also to all who have loved his appearing. *(2 Tim 4:7-8)*

You have need of endurance, so that you may do the will of God and receive what is promised. . . . Strive for peace with all men, and for the holiness without which no one will see the Lord. *(Heb 10:36; 12:14)*

We can only imagine all the extraordinary challenges Our Lady had encountered by the time she came to the end of her earthly life. So much she had endured, with courage, patience, perseverance, longsuffering — all the qualities of character that go to make up the virtue called *fortitude*.

In her assumption into heaven, Mary at last enjoyed the ripened fruit of a lifetime of endurance. Like St. Paul, she had fought the good fight, finished the race, and kept the faith. Through her endurance, she had been able to "do the will of God and receive what is promised": The holiest of women rose to heaven to see the Lord.

Our Lady's assumption was a special privilege set aside for the Mother of God. But in her heavenly destiny, we catch a glimpse of the glorious reward that St. Paul tells us is reserved for "all who have loved [Christ's] appearing." Mary has gone home before us, and she awaits us there.

With the Apostle, we long for what is mortal here on earth to be "swallowed up by life" in heaven (2 Cor 5:4). What a comfort, then, to know that at the end of a faithful journey — St. Paul promises — we, too, will be changed. Having become imperishable and immortal, we will reign in glory with Christ forever.

In the meantime, we must strive for holiness if we would see the Lord. To help us on the way, our Blessed Mother joins her Son in interceding for us, praying that all her children will receive the great grace of endurance.

Silent Reflection

- Our Father
- Ten Hail Marys
- Glory Be
- Fátima Prayer (optional)

The Fifth Glorious Mystery

THE CORONATION OF OUR LADY AS QUEEN OF HEAVEN

Spiritual Fruit: BEAUTY

When Christ who is our life appears, then you also will appear with him in glory.
COLOSSIANS 3:4

Christ loved the Church and gave himself up for her, that he might sanctify her, having cleansed her by the washing of water with the word, that he might present the Church to himself in splendor, without spot or wrinkle or any such thing, that she might be holy and without blemish. *(Eph 5:25-27)*

Finally, brethren, whatever is true, whatever is honorable, whatever is just, whatever is pure, whatever is lovely, whatever is gracious, if there is any excellence, if there is anything worthy of praise, think about these things. *(Phil 4:8)*

We come now to the last, and perhaps the sweetest, of the mysteries: Our Lord Jesus, the King of Heaven, delights to bestow on Our Lady, the Queen Mother, her rightful crown. It shines like the stars, and she is clothed in a royal robe dazzling like the sun, with the pale loveliness of the moon under her feet (see Rev 12:1).

In short, she is altogether beautiful in her splendor.

Say the word "glory," and our contemporaries most often think first of great renown. Foremost in the minds of the ancients, however, was the notion of glory as brilliant beauty. In fact, the biblical words often translated as "glory" might sometimes be better rendered as "splendor."

The Scripture passage speaks of God's "holy splendor," the gleaming beauty of His holiness (Ps 29:2; NAB). Those who reflect the resplendent light of His sanctity share in His loveliness. The holy man or woman is thus a "vessel for beauty" (Rom 9:21).

When we ponder the Glorious Mysteries, then, we are meditating on mysteries of breathtaking beauty — and none more beautiful than the coronation of Our Lady. In the crowning of Mary, Mother of the Church, we see fulfilled the words of St. Paul, for we see Christ "present the Church to himself in splendor, without spot or wrinkle or any such thing ... holy and without blemish."

The Apostle urges us to meditate on whatever is true, honorable, just, pure, lovely, gracious, excellent, or praiseworthy. These qualities belong to Mary in abundance. Whenever we reflect on her life in the Rosary, then, and on the life of her divine Son, we are heeding St. Paul's admonition.

Such meditation on these mysteries lights the way to eternity. We, too, become holy. We shimmer and glow. And at the last, we come to share Our Lady's beauty, set ablaze by the "Sun of Righteousness" himself (see Mal 4:2).

Silent Reflection

- Our Father
- Ten Hail Marys
- Glory Be
- Fátima Prayer (optional)

THE PRAYERS
OF THE ROSARY

Sign of the Cross

In the name of the Father, and of the Son, and of the Holy Spirit. Amen.

Apostles' Creed

I believe in God, the Father almighty, creator of heaven and earth; and in Jesus Christ, his only Son, our Lord; who was conceived by the Holy Spirit, born of the Virgin Mary, suffered under Pontius Pilate, was crucified, died, and was buried. He descended to the dead; the third day he arose again from the dead. He ascended into heaven and sits at the right hand of God, the Father almighty; from thence he shall come to judge the living and the dead. I believe in the Holy Spirit, the holy catholic Church, the communion of saints, the forgiveness of sins, the resurrection of the body, and life everlasting. Amen.

Our Father

Our Father, who art in heaven, hallowed be thy name. Thy kingdom come. Thy will be done on earth, as it is in heaven. Give us this day our daily bread, and forgive us our trespasses, as we forgive those who trespass against us, and lead us not into temptation, but deliver us from evil. Amen.

Hail Mary

Hail Mary, full of grace. The Lord is with thee. Blessed art thou among women, and blessed is the fruit of thy womb, Jesus. Holy Mary, Mother of God, pray for us sinners, now and at the hour of our death. Amen.

Glory Be

Glory be to the Father, and to the Son, and to the Holy Spirit. As it was in the beginning, is now, and ever shall be, world without end. Amen.

Fátima Prayer

O my Jesus, forgive us our sins, save us from the fires of hell. Lead all souls to heaven, especially those who have most need of your mercy. Amen.

Hail, Holy Queen

Hail, holy Queen, Mother of Mercy, our life, our sweetness, and our hope. To thee do we cry, poor banished children of Eve; to thee do we send up our sighs, mourning, and weeping in this valley of tears. Turn then, most gracious advocate, thine eyes of mercy toward us, and after this, our exile, show unto us the blessed fruit of thy womb, Jesus. O clement, O loving, O sweet Virgin Mary.

V. Pray for us, O Holy Mother of God.
R. That we may be made worthy of the promises of Christ.

Concluding Rosary Prayer

Let us pray: O God, whose only begotten Son, by his life, death, and resurrection, has purchased for us the rewards of eternal life, grant, we beseech thee, that meditating upon these mysteries of the Most Holy Rosary of the Blessed Virgin Mary, we may imitate what they contain and obtain what they promise, through the same Christ our Lord. Amen.

About the Author

Paul Thigpen, Ph.D., is professor of Sacred Theology at Southern Catholic College in Dawsonville, Georgia, and editor of *The Catholic Answer*, a national bimonthly magazine. He has published 36 books.